Contents

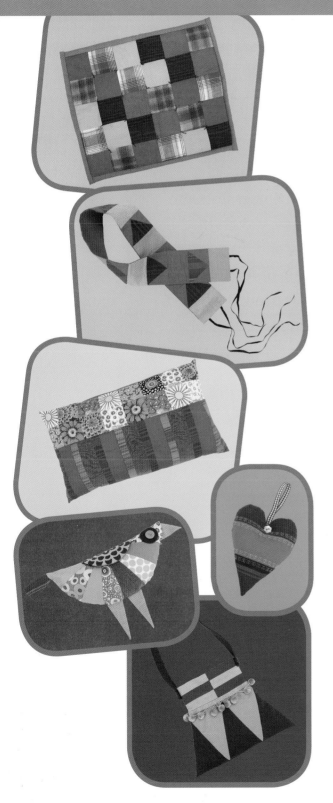

Introduction

From very early times people have made things to use up and reuse old clothes. Patchwork quilts were a way of recycling old clothes, as well as being a necessary source of warmth. Necessity makes for the best ideas! If you look at pictures of old patchwork quilts, you can see good examples of the fabrics used in the clothes of the time – patchwork has always been a great way to remember favourite garments. In the United States in the 19th century, groups of women would get together to finish their quilts, and these were called 'Quilting Bees'. The Shakers of America have provided us with wonderful inspiration which can be seen still today, using up scraps of their clothing.

FUNKY FACT! Fabric was precious to the early settlers of America. They wore their clothes until they fell apart, then cut them up to make patchwork from them.

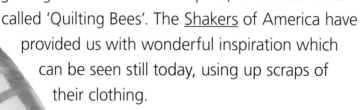

4

Start to
Patchwork

Nancy Nicholson

SEARCH PRESS

First published in Great Britain 2009
Search Press Ltd
Wellwood
North Farm Road
Tunbridge Wells
Kent TN2 3DR

Text copyright © Nancy Nicholson 2009

Photographs by Debbie Patterson at Search Press
Studios and by Roddy Paine Photographic Studios

Photographs and design copyright © Search Press Ltd
2009

*To my boys, Tom and Will, both of them
gifted creators.*

ISBN: 978-1-84448-264-1

Suppliers
If you have difficulty obtaining any of the materials
and equipment mentioned in this book, please visit the
Search Press website:
www.searchpress.com

Some words are underlined <u>like this</u>. They are
explained in the glossary on page 48.

The publishers would like to thank consultant,
Rebecca Vickers, and also the following for appearing in
the photographs: Georgia Brooks, Emily Murayama,
Lottie Brooks, Henrietta Amos, Chloe Barnard,
Rebekah Mate-Kole Rampe, Catherine Stevens,
Yuna Murayama, Amanda Abrahim,
Charlie de la Bédoyère and Abby Jeffery.
Thanks also to Sandy Paine and to Izzy and Daisy.

Printed in Malaysia

Today patchwork is still a great way to recycle. You can begin your collection of fabric straight away. Ask friends and family for old clothes or scraps of fabric they may have left over, or search in charity shops for interesting and colourful fabrics. It is fun building up your collection, and you should iron, fold and sort your fabric scraps to make designing easy.

I came to patchwork as a child, making dolls' clothes out of scraps of fabric given to me by my mother. I went on to make simple quilts, though it was collecting the materials as much as anything that I loved, and now I have bags and bags of scraps everywhere! I began with hand patchwork and loved cutting out the paper templates, gradually making enough to begin sewing them together. When my children were little, I made them many things, from toys and bibs to quilts and clothes. My oldest son loves to customise his own clothes and my youngest spends hours designing T-shirts and trainers. I hope you will love patchwork too!

Materials

Fabrics

You can use any scraps of dressmaking quality fabrics for most of the projects, though cotton is always best. Try to use the same weight of fabric for each individual project, as it will go together much more evenly and give a better finish. The Zigzag Bag on pages 42–47 uses heavier weight, upholstery fabric for a more winter weight style. For the Pet's Quilt on pages 12–17 and the Patchwork Pillow (pages 26–31) use a plain, coloured cotton fabric for the backing – it could even be an old sheet if it is a great colour!

Sewing equipment

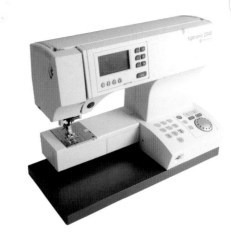

Sewing machine For most of the projects, you only need a machine that can do straight stitch. The Heart Decoration on pages 32–37 uses a heart-shaped machine embroidery stitch, but if your machine will not do this, you could embroider the piece by hand instead.

Scissors You will need a sharp pair of scissors to cut out the fabric accurately, and a smaller pair for snipping threads and more intricate cutting into corners.

Tape measure It is always a good idea to have a tape measure. If your measurements are correct, your work will go together much better.

Needles Needles for patchwork tend to be shorter, but a pack of assorted sewing needles will be fine.

Threads You will need a range of cotton sewing thread, both for the machine and for hand sewing. Some of the projects need the machine stitching to match the fabric used. You will also need some thick embroidery thread and some white tacking thread.

Pins Glass-headed pins or ordinary sewing pins can be used. If you can get some longer pins, they are useful for pinning the quilt layers together.

Pin cushion If you make the Pin Cushion project first (see page 18–21), you will have your first handmade piece of useful equipment!

Embellishments

You will need some pompoms, which are sold on a braid and are normally used to trim cushions and curtains; some scraps of ribbon for hanging loops, and some imitation suede lacing which you can get in good fabric stores or craft shops.

You will also need a variety of buttons for various projects. You can either find these at fabric stores or ask you friends and family if they have a button box for odd buttons.

Some projects use beads and sequins for decoration. Use seed beads or slightly bigger beads if you prefer. These come in many colours and can be found in craft and fabric shops.

Other materials

Plastic, card and brown paper for templates Ordinary brown parcel paper is useful for cutting out patterns. Where you need to make a stronger template, you can photocopy the patterns from the book, cut them out and draw round them on card. You can also trace patterns on to an old transparent plastic folder and cut them out.

Craft interfacing You can buy this in fabric stores. It comes in different weights, some for a stiffer effect, some lighter. It is used in the projects to slightly stiffen the fabric. Ensure that you iron with the rough side down on the wrong side of the fabric you are using.

Wadding This is used for the padding layer of quilts and is called 'batting' in the USA. The wadding used in the book is 2oz (56g) polyester wadding, which can be bought at good craft shops or online (see page 48).

Kapok filling You will need to buy a bag of kapok filling from a craft or fabric store.

Pillow inserts These can be any size you like, and can be bought in fabric stores or online.

Pens and pencils You will need a ballpoint pen and a soft pencil for drawing round your templates on to card and fabric.

Bias binding This comes in many colours and is used for a quick and simple edging. It could be used as an alternative edging for the Pet's Quilt on pages 12–17.

Techniques

Machine stitching

You can use a sewing machine to sew the patchwork pieces together.

1 Line up your fabric carefully. Use the gauge to set a 1cm (³/₈in) <u>seam allowance</u> and lower the machine's foot.

2 Set the machine to straight stitch. Press the foot pedal to sew.

3 When you have finished sewing, lift up the foot, slide out the sewn fabric and snip the threads.

Turning a corner

To turn a corner when machine sewing, stop at the corner with the needle in the fabric. Lift the foot, turn the piece you are sewing, put the foot down again and continue sewing.

Using craft interfacing

This is used to stiffen the fabric in some projects.

Cut out the craft interfacing and position it sticky side down on your fabric. Press it with a hot iron to attach it to the fabric.

Ladder stitch

This is very useful for sewing up the gaps that you leave in some pieces if you need to turn them right sides out and stuff them. You should do ladder stitch in a matching thread.

1 To sew up a gap in a piece, come up through the machine stitching to hide the knot inside the piece.

2 Make a small stitch along the fold on one side of the gap.

3 Pull through and make another small stitch along the fold on the other side of the gap. Continue until the whole gap is sewn up.

4 To fasten off, go back under the machine stitching and up again. Repeat several times and trim.

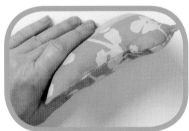

The finished seam.

Oversewing

You can also close up a gap by oversewing as shown below.

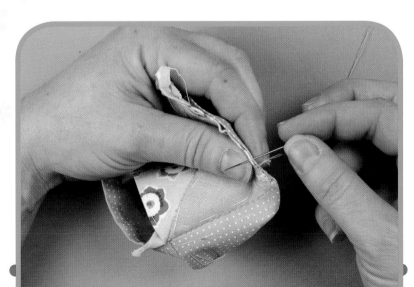

Thread a needle and knot the end of the thread. Bring the needle up from the wrong side of the fabric. Push the needle through the edges of both the pieces of fabric you are joining. Pull it through, then push the needle through again further along in the same direction, and so on until you have sewn together the edges. Fasten off by making several stitches on top of each other, then snip the ends.

Pet's Quilt

Make an adorable miniature quilt for your cat or dog, to line their basket. Choose bright colours which they will enjoy!

You will need

Paper or plastic for templates

Ballpoint pen or pencil

Six different fabric scraps for the patchwork top

Cotton backing fabric, 42cm (16½in) square

Four pieces of binding fabric: two 6 x 45cm (2³⁄₈ x 17¾in) and two 6 x 54cm, (2³⁄₈ x 21¼in) or bias binding

Sewing machine

Iron

Machine thread to contrast with your patchwork pieces

Wadding, 51cm (20in) square

Needle, pins, tacking thread, thread to match the binding fabric and thick, bright embroidery thread

I Make a 10cm (4in) square template from paper or plastic. Draw round it on six different fabrics and cut five squares from each fabric. I have cut out five pink, five yellow, five orange and five each in three different checked fabrics.

2 Lay the squares out in the pattern you have chosen for your quilt.

3 Pick up the squares one by one and stack them in a row on the right-hand side.

4 Thread up the sewing machine with contrasting thread (I have used red). Sew the top square from the first stack to the second square. Place the squares right sides together and sew along one side with a 1cm ($^3/_8$in) seam allowance.

5 Sew the third square to the second square in the same way and continue through the whole stack to make one row. Then sew the second stack in the same way, and so on. Iron the seams open, then iron the front of each row.

6 Place two rows right sides together and match up the seams carefully. Machine sew along a long edge with a 1cm ($^3/_8$in) seam allowance.

7 Continue in this way, sewing each row to the next row. When the quilt front is all sewn together, iron the seams open as before. Iron the front as well.

8 Layer the backing fabric, then the wadding, then the front piece. Line them up carefully.

9 Pin the three layers in place as shown. Place a pin in each corner and one in the middle, then one in the middle of each side.

10 Thread a needle with tacking thread. Starting in the middle of one side, tack across the middle to the other side. Repeat across the middle in the other direction. Then tack along each edge as shown.

11 Fold down the long edge of a binding piece 1cm (³/₈in) and iron it down. Repeat the other side. Do this for all four binding pieces.

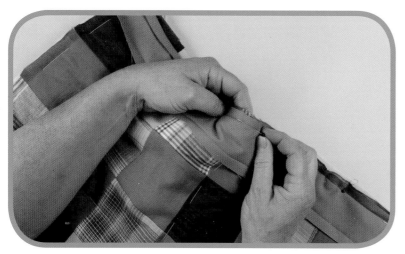

12 Place a long binding piece right sides together along a long edge of the quilt and pin along the fold.

13 Tack along the fold line. Thread up the machine with matching thread and sew with a 1cm (³/₈in) seam allowance. Repeat steps 12 and 13 for the other long edge.

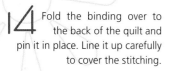

14 Fold the binding over to the back of the quilt and pin it in place. Line it up carefully to cover the stitching.

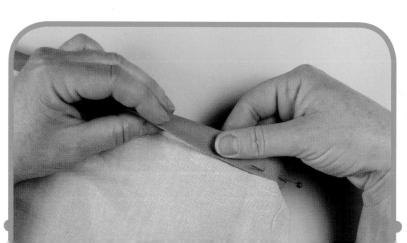

15 Tack the binding in place and remove the pins. Oversew with matching thread. Repeat steps 14 and 15 to complete both long edges.

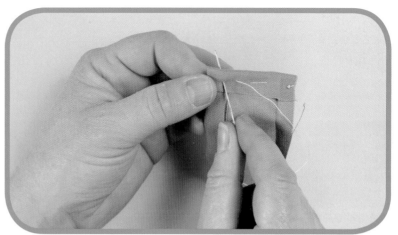

16 Fold down the end of a shorter binding piece and tack it in place with one side folded down and one side open as shown.

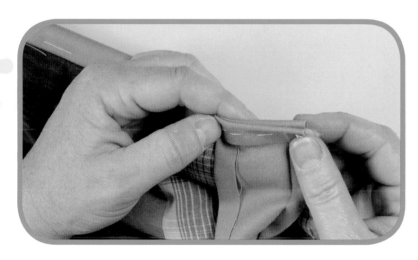

17 Line up the folded end with the end of a long bound edge of the quilt as shown. Pin the binding down the short edge along the fold as before.

18 At the other end, cut off any excess binding, leaving a 1cm (³/₈in) overhang.

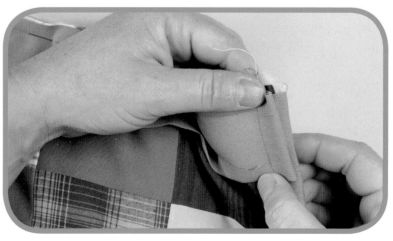

19 Fold back the end as in step 17. Tack the binding on as for the long sides.

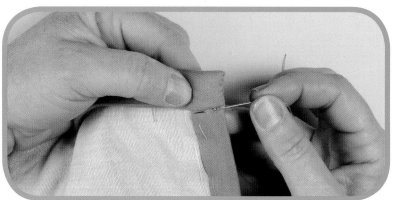

20 Machine sew along the short edge as before. Repeat steps 16 to 20 for the other short edge.

21 Turn over the binding to the back of the quilt, then tack into position. Oversew along the corner, then turn the quilt and oversew along the short edge as before. Take the tacking stitches out and trim all the ends of thread.

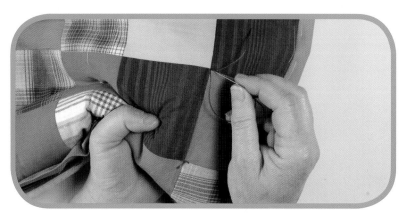

22 Thread a needle with bright, thick embroidery thread. Go in from the front of the quilt into a point between squares. Leave a 6cm (2³/₈in) tail. Come up 5mm (¼in) away and go down where you first came up.

23 Come up again, trim the thread to a 6cm (2³/₈in) tail and knot the two tails. Knot two more times and trim the ends. Make a similar knot at all the points between squares.

What next?

Try making a bigger quilt as a cover for your bed. You could even put some simple <u>appliqué shapes</u> on the squares before you sew them together.

Pin Cushion

This is such a quick and easy project to make and you can use your pin cushion for all your other patchwork projects. Once you have made one pin cushion, you will want to try other combinations of fabric and shapes.

The patterns for the Pin Cushion, shown three quarters of actual size. You will need to enlarge them to 133% on a photocopier.

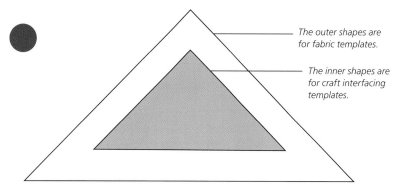

The outer shapes are for fabric templates.

The inner shapes are for craft interfacing templates.

TOP TIP!

As long as you cut out your pin cushion pieces accurately, they should fit together beautifully.

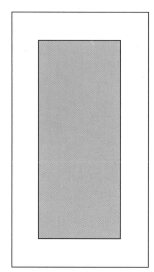

1 Photocopy the patterns, cut them out and draw round them on card to make templates. Draw round the templates on fabric to make two large patterned triangles, two plain triangles, four rectangles and one square.

2 Make smaller card templates from the inner shapes of the patterns. Draw round them on craft interfacing and cut out four rectangles, four triangles and a square.

3 Place the craft interfacing shapes face down on the back of the fabric shapes and iron them down, leaving an even border around them.

4 Thread a needle with a single thread and knot the end. Fold down the edge of a shape over the craft interfacing and tack it in place. When you get to the next side, fold it down and do a stitch over the overlap to hold the corner down. Tack round all the pieces in this way.

5 Lay a patterned and a plain triangle side by side as shown, then place them right sides together. Thread a needle with a matching thread and knot the end. Come up through both triangles and oversew along the edge (see page 11).

6 At the other end, sew over the same spot three or four times to secure the stitching, then trim the thread.

7 Sew together the other two triangles in the same way, then sew the two pairs together. Match up the seams carefully as shown and start sewing in the middle.

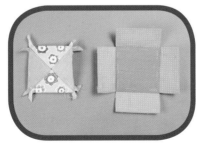

8 Sew the rectangles to the square in the same way so that you have a flattened box shape and a lid shape as shown.

9 Stitch up the short sides of two of the rectangles with the craft interfacing on the outside (or 'wrong sides out'). You will begin to see a three-dimensional box shape.

10 Turn the box shape right sides out as shown.

11 To attach the lid, place it right sides together against one side of the box. Oversew the edges together.

12 Sew up the next side of the box. This time you will have to work right sides out, so make tiny stitches as they will show.

13 Sew up the next side in the same way, then leave the last side open for stuffing, leaving the needle attached. Stuff the pin cushion firmly with kapok, pushing it into the corners.

14 Sew up the final edge with tiny oversewing stitches.

15 Snip the tacking stitches with sharp scissors and pull them out.

What next?

You can make these colourful pin cushions in so many ways. Be inventive with your fabric choices. Stripes can make exciting, almost 3D patterns!

Beautiful Belt

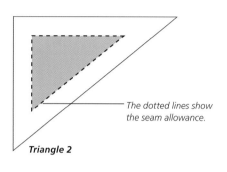

This versatile belt will brighten up any outfit, whether just jeans or a dress.

The patterns for the Beautiful Belt, shown half actual size. You will need to enlarge them to 200% on a photocopier.

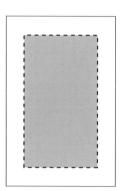

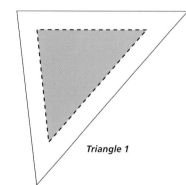

The dotted lines show the seam allowance.

Triangle 2

Triangle 1

1 Photocopy the patterns, draw round them on card and cut them out to make templates. Draw round the templates on your fabric.

2 Cut out three rectangles each in three different colours of fabric; four each of triangle 1 in two different striped fabrics and eight each of triangle two in two colours, as shown.

3 Take a triangle 1 in the first striped fabric and lay a triangle 2 on top as shown, right sides together, with an equal overhang at each end.

4 Thread up the sewing machine with matching thread in the top and the bobbin and sew along the edge with a 1cm (^{3}/$_8$in) seam allowance.

5 Sew all the striped triangle 1 shapes to the pink triangle 2 shapes in the same way.

6 Sew the orange triangles to the left-hand sides of the other striped triangle 1 shapes. Press the seams open with your fingers and carefully iron them flat.

7 Each triangle 1 now needs to have the opposite coloured triangle 2 on its other side. Place each triangle 2 right sides together against the right-hand edge with an equal overhang each side as shown.

8 Sew the second triangles in place by machine, leaving a 1cm (^{3}/$_8$in) seam allowance as before.

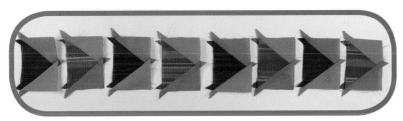

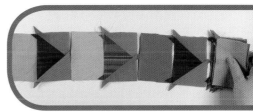

9 Iron all the seams open, then iron all the right sides, and lay out all the patchworked triangles as shown.

10 Place the plain rectangles between the patchworked triangles in sequence. Stack all the pieces in sequence.

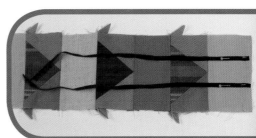

11 Machine sew the rectangles to the patchworked triangles with a 1cm (^{3}/$_8$in) seam allowance. Iron the seams open and iron the front as well.

12 Cut out a lining to fit the belt, 10 x 89cm (4 x 35in). Take the two strips of craft interfacing, place them sticky side down on the back of the belt and on the lining, and iron them on.

13 Take four pieces of imitation suede lacing, each 33cm (13in) long and pin them on either end of the front of the belt, as shown.

14 Place the lining and the belt right sides together and pin them.

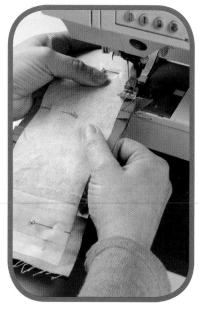

15 Start one third of the way down a long side and machine sew along the edge of the craft interfacing. Sew all round the edge, leaving one third open in the middle of the edge you started with. Turn corners as shown on page 10.

16 Take out the pins and snip off the corners and the overhanging bits of triangles.

TOP TIP!

Remember that snipping the corners carefully will give the belt a professional finish.

17 Turn the belt right sides out and push the corners out using closed, blunt scissors.

18 Fold the edges of the gap over the craft interfacing. Iron them down and pin them.

19 Thread a needle with doubled matching thread. Come up from the inside to hide the knot and sew up the gap using ladder stitch (see page 11).

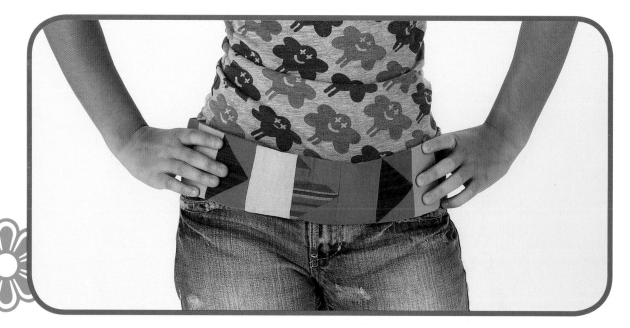

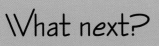

What next?

Try using different patterned fabrics which will make completely different effects depending on how you arrange them. You could also embellish your belt with beads and sequins!

25

Patchwork Pillow

This wonderfully modern pillow is so simple and quick to make, and can be given as a gift or used to brighten your bedroom!

You will need

Clear plastic and brown paper for templates

Ballpoint pen

Scissors

Five different flowered fabrics and plain and striped fabrics for stalks

Sewing machine and threads to match fabrics

Iron

Pins

Two pieces of backing fabric, each 50 x 22cm (19¾ x 8¾in)

Pillow insert, 48 x 27cm (19 x 10⅝in)

1 Make 8cm (3¹/₈in) square templates from clear plastic. This means that you can choose good areas of your flowery fabric before drawing round the templates. Cut out sixteen flowered squares from a variety of fabrics. I have used five fabrics.

2 Make stalk templates from brown paper, one 18 x 6cm (7 x 2³/₈in) and one 18 x 4cm (7 x 1½in). Draw round the templates and cut out ten narrow stalks and seven wide stalks in four different fabrics.

3 Lay out the squares in two rows in a repeat pattern, and the stalks underneath. Alternate wide and narrow stalks but have narrow ones at either end. This is a chance for you to work out how you want your patchwork pillow to look.

4 Pick up the patchwork pieces one by one and make a stack for each row.

STAY SAFE

Always ask an adult to help you set up the sewing machine.

5 Take the first two squares from the stack and place them right sides together. Match up the edges carefully. Thread up the sewing machine with matching thread. I have used pale green on the top and in the bobbin. Set the gauge for a 1cm (³/₈in) seam allowance and sew along one side to join the squares. Lift the foot, pull out the piece and trim the threads.

6 Sew together the whole row in this way, then iron the seams open.

7 Sew together the second row of squares in the same way. Then place the first and second rows right sides together, matching up the seams carefully, and machine sew them together with a 1cm (³/₈in) seam allowance.

8 Iron this seam open.

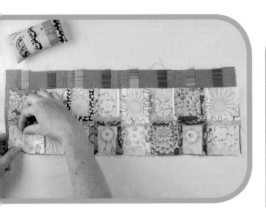

9 Sew the stalks together in the same way. Line up the patchworked stalks and the patchworked squares and place them right sides together. Pin them in place.

10 Machine sew the stalks and the squares together with a 1cm (³/₈in) seam allowance. Make sure the seams are still open back and front, and remove the pins as you go.

11 Iron the new seam open.

TOP TIP!

Ironing the seams flat at each stage will make all the difference to how well the patchwork pieces go together.

12 Iron the front of the piece and trim any edges that need to be evened up.

13 Take a backing piece. Turn over the long edge 1cm (³/₈in) and iron it down.

14 Turn the edge over again and iron again. Repeat for the other backing piece.

15 Thread the sewing machine with matching thread in the top and bobbin. Sew along the folded edge close to the fold. Sew both pieces.

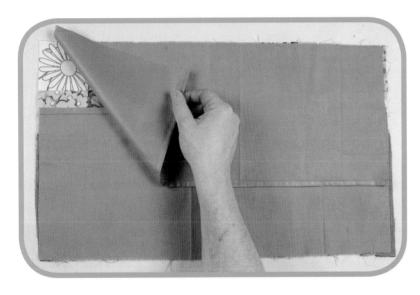

16 Place the pillow case front right side up. Place one backing piece on top with the folded edge upwards, and the second piece on top of that with the folded edge downwards.

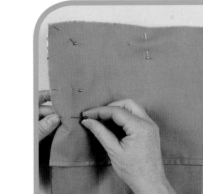

17 Pin all the way round the edge of the pillow case.

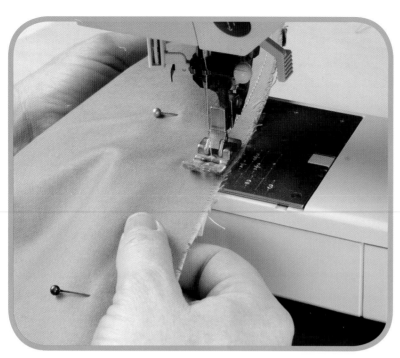

18 Sew all the way round the edges of the pillow case with a 1cm ($^3/_8$in) seam allowance. Turn the corners as shown on page 10.

19 Take out the pins. Trim the corners by cutting across them diagonally from each side. Do not cut as far as the stitching.

20 Turn the pillow case right sides out and push out the corners with closed scissors. Put in the pillow insert to complete your patchwork pillow.

What next?

Make covers for pillows you have at home. Fabrics in contrasting colours look great. Try different ways of laying out the patchwork pieces, such as alternating floral and plain fabrics.

Heart Decoration

These decorations will look wonderful at any time of year hanging from a mantelpiece or elsewhere around the home.

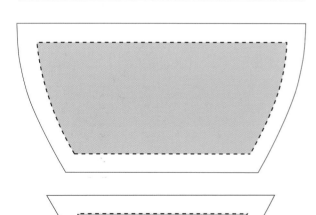

You will need

Card or brown paper for templates

Iron

Ballpoint pen or soft pencil

Striped and plain fabric

Scissors

Sewing machine and threads to match and contrast with fabrics

Medium-weight craft interfacing

Pins and needle

Kapok filling

Ribbon, 25cm (10in) long

Two buttons

The patterns for the Heart Decoration, shown half actual size. You will need to enlarge them to 200% on a photocopier.

The pattern for the craft interfacing template.

The dotted lines show the seam allowance.

1 Photocopy the patterns, cut out the shapes and draw round them on card or brown paper to make templates. Iron the fabric and draw round the templates on your chosen fabric.

2 Cut out two shapes for the top of the heart and two for the bottom in striped fabric, and two for the middle in plain fabric.

3 Place a top and a middle piece right sides together, matching up the edges carefully.

4 Thread the sewing machine with matching thread in the top and the bobbin. Set the gauge to a 1cm ($^3/_8$in) seam allowance and sew the pieces together.

5 Line up the bottom of the heart, right sides together, with the middle.

6 Sew the middle and the bottom together as in step 3.

7 Repeat steps 3 to 6 to make the other side of the heart. Open out the seams at the back of the heart and iron them flat. Iron the front of each piece as well.

8 Make a template from the smaller heart shape and draw round it on craft interfacing.

9 Place the craft interfacing sticky side down on the back of a heart and iron it on. Repeat with the other heart.

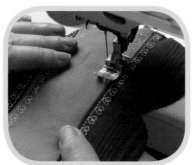

10 Choose a contrasting coloured thread (I have used a very pale green) and thread up the sewing machine top. Select an embroidery pattern on your machine (I have used a heart). Sew a line of embroidery either side of each seam.

11 Repeat with the other heart. Place the two embroidered heart pieces right sides together, matching the seams carefully.

12 Pin the pieces together. Place the pins horizontally as shown. Thread up the machine with matching thread top and bottom and change it back to straight stitch. Begin sewing round the edge of the craft interfacing, starting at the bottom of the top section.

13 Sew round the curve to the centre point. Leave the needle in, lift the foot and turn the piece ready to stitch the other curve.

14 Lower the foot again and sew right round the heart, repeating step 13 at the bottom point. Sew to the bottom of the middle section near where you started, leaving the middle section open. Pull the piece out of the machine and snip the threads.

15 Snip diagonally across each side of the bottom point. Do not snip right up to the machine stitching.

16 Make little snips into the curves, but again do not cut as far as the machine stitching. Snip a 'v' shape in towards the centre point.

17 Fold back the edges around the opening you have left in the middle section.

18 Thread a needle with a single tacking thread and do running stitch along each folded back piece to hold them in place. Do not sew up the gap.

19 Turn the heart right sides out and push out the point with closed scissors. Stroke all the seams with the closed scissors.

20 Stuff kapok into the curves and the point first, then fill the heart a handful at a time.

21 Sew up the gap using ladder stitch (see page 11). Thread a needle with doubled, matching thread, knot the end and come up through the machine stitching. Make a stitch along the fold on one side.

22 Pull through and make a stitch along the fold on the other side. Do not pull the thread too tight or the heart will be puckered. Continue until you have sewn up the gap.

23 To fasten off, sew over the two sides several times in the same place.

24 Take the needle down and out into the front of the heart to hide the tail of thread inside. Trim very closely. Take out the tacking stitches.

25 Take 25cm (10in) of ribbon and cut diagonally across each end.

26 Knot the end of a matching doubled thread and come up between the curves of the heart. Make a couple of stitches through both sides. Fold the ribbon in half and take the needle through the ribbon ends.

27 Do a couple of stitches through the heart and the ribbon ends to hold the ribbon in place. Take two buttons. Go through a button and back though the heart and ribbon, then through the other button on the other side. Repeat several times.

28 To fasten off, wrap the thread around the base of a button four times. Go down under the button and come up in the middle of the work to conceal the thread ends.

29 Pull through and snip the thread ends.

What next?

Try different shapes, like diamonds or triangles. You could also decorate your shapes with hand embroidery, beads or sequins.

Crazy Bird

This colourful bird can be made in many sizes, in fact you could make a whole family!

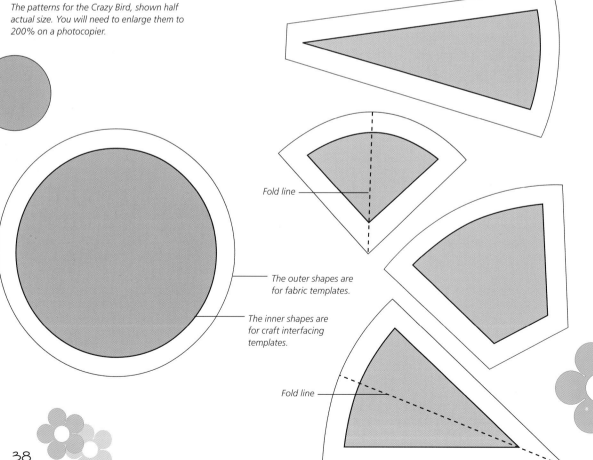

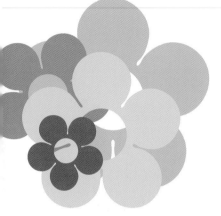

The patterns for the Crazy Bird, shown half actual size. You will need to enlarge them to 200% on a photocopier.

Fold line

The outer shapes are for fabric templates.

The inner shapes are for craft interfacing templates.

Fold line

1 Make a small and a large template for each shape using card or brown paper. Use the larger ones to cut out: two body pieces each in eight different fabrics; one wing in each of two fabrics; two leg pieces in one fabric; two tail pieces in one fabric and one piece for the beak.

2 Use the smaller templates to cut out a craft interfacing shape for each of the pieces in step 1.

3 Place the craft interfacing pieces sticky side down on the backs of the fabric pieces and iron them down.

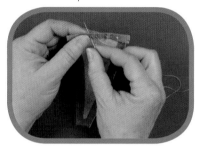

4 Take a body piece and fold back the fabric edge over the craft interfacing. Fold carefully so that you retain the shape of the curved edge. Thread a needle with a single tacking thread and knot the end. Tack round all the folded down edges.

5 Repeat for all the body pieces. Place two pieces right sides together. Thread the needle with matching thread and knot the end. Sew the pieces together along a long edge with neat oversewing (see page 11).

6 Sew together eight different body parts in this way, then sew together the other eight in the same order to make the other side of the bird. Snip and pull out the tacking stitches you made in step 4.

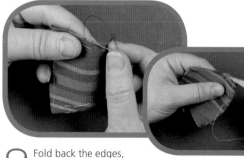

7 Fold down the edges of each wing piece as in step 4 and tack round them, keeping a neat curve.

8 Thread the needle with a matching thread. Place the wing pieces wrong sides together and use matching thread to oversew around the edges, leaving a 6cm (2½in) gap.

9 Fold back the edges, tack and sew the tail in the same way, wrong sides together. Snip the knots of the wing and tail pieces and take out the tacking stitches.

10 Fold back and tack the straight edges of the beak and leg pieces. Fold the beak piece in half, bringing the straight edges together. Oversew the straight edges together with matching thread. Do not sew up the curve. Repeat for the two legs.

11 Place the two sides of the bird's body right sides together, matching the seams. Machine sew along the straight edge with a 1cm (³/₈in) seam allowance and matching thread.

12 Iron the piece.

13 Place the wing circle centrally over the body piece, with half of it either side of the seam. Machine sew it in place.

14 Pin and tack the beak, legs and tail in place as shown.

15 Ladder stitch the pieces in place (see page 11).

16 Place the eye next to the beak. Thread a needle with contrasting thread, come up from the back through the eye and the button, go back down and repeat several times.

17 Fasten off at the back by oversewing several stitches on top of one another.

18 Sew on the other eye on the other side of the bird's central seam.

19 Fold the bird in half, matching the seams, and begin to ladder stitch around the edge, starting at the tail end.

20 When you reach a leg, ladder stitch along the unsewn side to secure it.

21 Sew past the second leg in the same way, then stop and fasten off. Start again at the head end and ladder stitch the beak in the same way as the legs.

22 Leave an opening of 8cm (3¼in). Stuff the bird with kapok filling, then use ladder stitch to close the opening. Remove all the tacking stitches.

What next?

Make a bigger bird as a crazy pillow for your room, or choose brighter fabrics and add sequins for an even crazier, more exotic bird.

Zigzag Bag

This original bag will look great over your shoulder. You could choose fabrics so that it goes with your favourite outfit.

You will need

Brown paper for templates

Ballpoint pen or soft pencil

Scissors

Light, dark, blue and red plain upholstery or thicker cotton fabrics

Pins

Sewing machine and threads to match fabrics

Iron

Pompom fringe

Lining fabric, 1m x 40cm (39½ x 15¾in)

Fabric for handle, 76 x 8cm (30 x 3¼in)

Two large buttons

Needle and tacking thread

The patterns for the Zigzag Bag shown half actual size. You will need to enlarge them to 200% on a photocopier.

The dotted lines show the seam allowance.

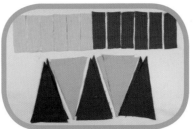

I | Make templates from the larger shapes and use them to cut out fabric shapes.

2 | Cut out six large triangles in a dark colour and four in a contrasting light colour. Cut out six rectangles in pale blue and six in red.

3 | Line up a light and a dark triangle as shown, with an equal overhang at each end.

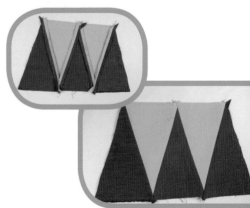

5 | Thread up the machine with matching thread top and bottom. With a 1cm (³⁄₈in) seam allowance, sew across the long edge.

4 | Pin the pieces together as shown.

6 | Open up the seam and iron it flat.

7 | Iron the front of the piece as well.

8 | Sew the other triangles to these first two in the same way to complete one side of the bag. Repeat steps 3 to 8 to make the other side.

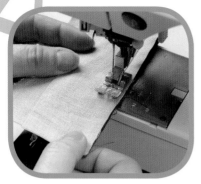 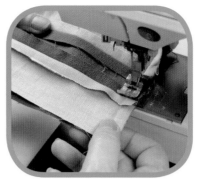 

9 Sew together three rectangles, long side to long side in the sequence blue-red-blue. Then sew together the other three in the sequence red-blue-red. Line up the edges carefully and iron the seams flat after you have sewn each one.

10 Put the two sets of three right sides together and match up the seams carefully. Machine sew them together along the shorter edge.

11 Iron the seam flat.

12 Iron the right sides as well. This completes one side of the bag's top section. Repeat steps 9 to 11 to make the other side of the bag top.

13 Put a top section right sides together with a bottom section of the bag. Match up the seams and pin.

  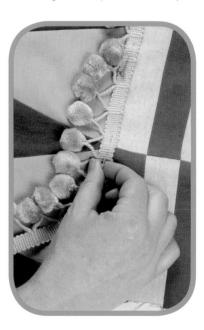

14 Set the machine to a 1cm (3/8in) seam allowance and sew the top to the bottom section.

15 Iron the seam open, then iron the front as well. Repeat steps 13 to 15 to make the other side of the bag.

16 Pin the pompom fringe along the seam joining the top and bottom sections of the bag.

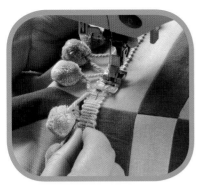

17 Thread up the sewing machine with matching thread and sew the fringe on to the seam with one row of stitching. Pull out the pins as you go. Repeat for the other side of the bag.

18 Draw round one side of the bag on the lining fabric and cut out the shape. Repeat to make the other side of the lining.

19 Place a lining piece over a bag piece, right sides together and pin in place.

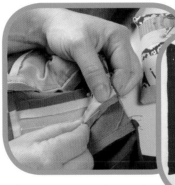

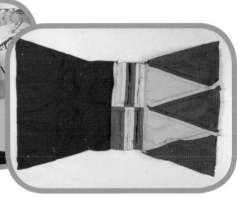

20 Thread up the machine with a top thread to match and sew across the top edges to attach the lining to the bag. Repeat for the other side of the bag. Open out and iron the seams.

21 Place the bag front and back right sides together, carefully lining up the seams, and pin.

The bag front and back, with linings attached, pinned together.

22 Begin sewing on the end of the linings, 12cm (4¾in) from the corner. Turn the corners as shown on page 10.

23 Sew all the way round the bag and lining, leaving a 14cm (5½in) gap in the end of the lining. Make sure that the opened seams remain flat as you sew over them, and be careful not to trap the pompoms in the stitching.

24 Trim across all four corners to make the shape neater when the bag is right sides out.

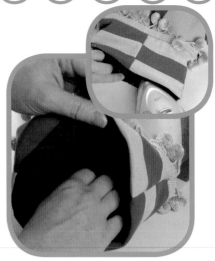

25 Pull the bag through the gap in the opening. Push out all the corners with closed scissors.

26 Iron the opening flat and machine sew across the opening, close to the folded edge.

27 Push the lining inside the bag. Iron the bag, especially at the top where the lining is attached.

28 Take the fabric for the handle. Fold in 7mm (½in) all the way round and iron it in place. Thread a needle with a single thread, knot the end and tack round the edges.

29 Fold the handle in half lengthwise, iron it flat, then pin it in place.

30 Thread up the machine with matching thread and set the gauge to 3mm (⅛in). Sew along the end, the long edge and the other end, turning the corners as on page 10.

31 Thread a needle with matching thread. Place the handle end over the bag's side seam, centred 3cm (1¼in) from the top. Place a button on top. Come up from the inside of the bag and go through the handle and button, then go back down through the handle and button. Continue in this way, sewing the handle and button to the bag.

32 Fasten off by sewing several stitches on top of one another in the lining inside the bag. Repeat the other side of the bag to complete the attaching of the handle.

What next?

Make the same bag with
flowery and striped fabrics.
You could also try making a
miniature bag for parties and
add some sparkle with beads
and sequins.

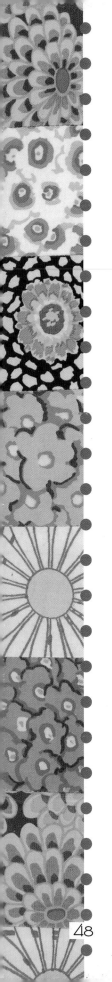

More books to read

Patchwork, Quilting and Appliqué by Linda Seward, Mitchell Beazley, 1996
The Encyclopedia of Quilting and Patchwork Techniques by Kathleen Guerrier, Dover Books, 2001
Material Obsession: Contemporary quilt designs by Kathy Doughty and Sarah Fielke, Murdoch Books, 2008
Kaffe Fassett Patchwork: Over 25 Glorious Designs, Ebury Press, 1997
Making History: Quilts & Fabric from 1890–1970 by Barbara Brackman, C & T Publishing, 2008

Useful websites

www.americanmuseum.org
www.cottonpatch.co.uk (for a great range of fabrics and other patchwork tools, plus books)
www.design-a-cushions.co.uk
www.qualityfibres.co.uk
www.reprodepot.com
www.joann.com

Glossary

Appliqué shapes Fabric shapes that are attached to a fabric surface by sewing or other methods.
Seam allowance This is the distance between the cut edges of the fabric and the stitching when you sew two pieces of fabric together. You can set the gauge on your sewing machine for the seam allowance that you want.
Shakers A protestant religious group that began in England in 1747 and later set up communities in America. They became well known for their furniture and quilts.

Index